Pink Princess CUPCAKES

Barbara Beery

PHOTOGRAPHY BY ZAC WILLIAMS

GIBBS SMITH
TO ENRICH AND INSPIRE HUMANKIND

Salt Lake City | Charleston | Santa Fe | Santa Barbara

First Edition
14 13 12 11 10   10 9 8 7 6 5 4 3 2 1

Published by
Gibbs Smith
P.O. Box 667
Layton, Utah 84041

1.800.835.4993 orders
www.gibbs-smith.com

Designed by Dawn DeVries Sokol
Manufactured in Shenzhen, China in October 2009 by Toppan Printing Co. (SZ) Ltd.
Gibbs Smith books are printed on either recycled, 100% post-consumer waste,
FSC-certified papers or on paper produced from a 100% certified sustainable
forest/controlled wood source.

The safety of our children is the most important ingredient in teaching kids to cook.
Children of all ages should be assisted by an adult while working in the kitchen and
making any recipe in this cookbook. The publisher and author assume no responsibility
for any damages or injuries incurred while making any of the recipes in this book.

Library of Congress Cataloging-in-Publication Data

Beery, Barbara, 1954–
  Pink princess cupcakes / Barbara Beery ; photography by Zac Williams. — 1st ed.
    p. cm.
  ISBN-13: 978-1-4236-0738-0
  ISBN-10: 1-4236-0738-4
  1. Cupcakes—Juvenile literature. I. Title.
  TX771.B39 2009
  641.8'653—dc22
                            2009026444

Contents

Cupcakes

Baking Tips

Welcome to cupcake camp! Here you'll learn tips and tricks to make, bake, and decorate the perfect cupcake. We'll talk about cupcake flavors and additions, baking in liners and molds, and how to measure and mix, bake and cool, and frost and decorate your cupcakes.

Cupcake Flavors and Additions

• Use any of the five delicious homemade cupcake recipes in this cookbook. You can always use your favorite cake mix to make cupcakes too. These recipes and most boxed cake mixes make 20 to 24 cupcakes.

• Fruit juices work especially well to add a natural sweetness, moistness, and fruit flavor to cupcakes. You can add fruit juice to almost any vanilla or fruit-flavored cupcake recipe by substituting the milk or water called for with an equal amount of fruit juice.

• Make specialty cupcake flavors by folding "stir-ins" into your cupcake batter after it has been mixed. Fun stir-ins include colorful sprinkles, mini chocolate chips, crushed hard candies, marshmallows, or whatever else you think would be good.

Cupcake Liners and Molds

• You can dress up your cupcakes with colorful paper and foil cupcake liners. They are festive and inexpensive, and they make cleanup a snap!

• Bright and colorful silicone cupcake molds are another perfect choice for cupcake liners. Not only do they come in a variety of whimsical shapes, but they are also an eco-friendly baking choice because the molds may be washed and used over and over.

• For a large selection of colorful paper cupcake liners and silicone cupcake molds, visit www. kidscookingshop.com.

• To make sure your baked cupcakes do not stick to the liners, lightly spray the inside of each liner with nonstick cooking spray before adding the batter.

Measure and Mix

- Carefully measure all ingredients. Dry ingredients like flour and sugar should be measured in measuring cups that are specifically made for dry ingredients. Just scoop dry ingredients loosely into measuring cups and level off the top with the back of a table knife. Liquid ingredients like milk and oil should be measured in clear measuring cups with spouts that are specifically made for measuring liquid ingredients. Place the measuring cup on the counter and then bend down and look at the cup at eye level to make sure your measurement is correct.
- Bring all ingredients such as eggs, liquids, and butter to room temperature before making your cupcake batter. The ingredients will mix more evenly and the result will be a wonderfully smooth and creamy cupcake batter.
- Don't overmix the batter. This will cause the cupcakes to become chewy and tough rather than perfectly moist and tender.

- Fill cupcake cups one-half to two-thirds full. Try using an ice cream scoop to fill the cupcake cups—every scoop is the same amount, so each cupcake will be the perfect size every time!

Bake and Cool

- Always remember to preheat your oven to the correct temperature before putting your cupcakes in to bake. When the oven is ready, gently place the cupcakes inside and then set your timer for the minimum baking time suggested in the recipe.
- When the timer goes off, test for doneness by sticking a clean toothpick in the center of a cupcake. If it comes out clean, the cupcakes are ready. If not, let them continue to bake in the oven and set the timer for the additional minutes suggested in the bake time. Then test again.
- Make sure you have two 12-cup cupcake pans or one 24-cup cupcake pan available. Having one or the other will ensure you'll have enough

room to make one batch of cupcakes. Never put cupcake batter into a warm cupcake pan because the cupcakes will bake unevenly and be lopsided.

- For easier and safer handling, put your cupcake pan on a cookie sheet. Bake only one pan of cupcakes at a time and place the pan in the very center of the oven. You can rotate your pan halfway through baking time to ensure that all cupcakes bake and brown evenly.

- When cupcakes are done, carefully remove them from the oven using an oven mitt or hot pad. Gently place cupcake pan on a cooling rack for 5 minutes. Remove cupcakes from the pan and then place each cupcake back onto the cooling rack for 30 minutes.

- Cupcakes are best eaten the same day they are made—and who doesn't want to eat cupcakes right away? Undecorated cupcakes may be frozen, covered, for up to 3 months.

Frost and Decorate

- Before you begin frosting cupcakes, brush the top of each one lightly with your fingers or use a dry pastry brush to remove any loose crumbs.

- Add some fanciful fun to your frosting by adding either a "touch" or a "bunch" of color with paste food dyes. Paste food dyes have a much truer and intense color than liquid food dyes. A tiny bit goes a long way in a batch of frosting.

- If you prefer all-natural food dyes, there are several companies that make a complete line of all-natural food dyes and candy decorations. Visit www.kidscookingshop.com to check the best options available.

- To frost cupcakes, spoon a heaping tablespoon of frosting onto the center of each cupcake. Use a table knife, a small plastic picnic knife, or a craft stick to spread and smooth the frosting. Just start in the center and move towards the outer edges of each cupcake. Keep the frosting piled high in the center of the cupcakes. Sometimes, you may even need to add a little more!

- There are endless possibilities for decorating cupcakes! Classic decorations for cupcakes range from colorful decorating sugars, sprinkles, and jimmies to gummy bears,

M&M's, Lifesavers, and jelly beans.
- Purchased cookies such as Oreos, vanilla wafers, gingersnaps, animal crackers, and Teddy Grahams work beautifully as cupcake toppers.

- Try pretzel twists or pretzel sticks— plain or dipped in chocolate and decorated with sprinkles.
- Popcorn and miniature marshmallows also make a festive choice to top cupcakes.

Cupcake Recipes

Following are five delicious homemade cupcake recipes. The suggested combinations of cupcake flavors, frostings, and decorations used in the themed cupcake recipes that follow are both scrumptious and beautiful. But please feel free to change the cupcake flavors and frostings to best suit the tastes of your family and friends.

Each cupcake recipe calls for self-rising flour and superfine granulated sugar. These ingredients were specifically chosen because they ensure both light and moist cupcakes. If you do not have these items, you can easily transform what you have on hand. Just follow these instructions:

Turn All-Purpose Flour into Self-Rising Flour

Add 1½ teaspoons baking powder and ¼ teaspoon salt to 1 cup all-purpose flour. Combine with a whisk and store in an airtight container.

Turn Granulated Sugar into Superfine Granulated Sugar

Place 1 cup granulated sugar into a food processor or blender and whirl for 30 seconds to break down the sugar crystals into smaller ones.

Note: Remember to measure the amount of sugar in a recipe *after* you have changed the granulated sugar into superfine granulated sugar.

Favorite Vanilla Cupcakes

Makes 20 to 24

1⅓ cups unsalted butter,
    room temperature
1½ cups superfine granulated sugar
6 large eggs, room temperature
2 teaspoons vanilla extract
3 cups self-rising flour

1 Preheat oven to 350 degrees F.
Lightly spray the inside of each cupcake
liner or mold with nonstick cooking
spray. Set aside.

2 In a large bowl, cream together the
butter and sugar with a hand mixer
until light and fluffy.

3 Beat in eggs, one at a time, mixing
well after each addition. Stir in vanilla.
Add flour, 1 cup at a time, mixing after
each addition until just blended.

4 Fill each liner or mold one-half to
two-thirds full of batter. Bake for
15 to 20 minutes.

5 Carefully remove cupcake pan from
oven and place on a cooling rack for
5 minutes. Remove cupcakes from pan

and place back on the rack to cool for 30
minutes before frosting and decorating.

Choco-licious Cupcakes

Makes 20 to 24

1½ cups unsalted butter,
    room temperature
1½ cups superfine granulated sugar
6 large eggs, room temperature
2 teaspoons vanilla extract
1 teaspoon coconut extract
2 cups self-rising flour
1 cup cocoa powder
2 tablespoons hot water

1 Preheat oven to 375 degrees F.
Lightly spray the inside of each cupcake
liner or mold with nonstick cooking
spray. Set aside.

2 In a large bowl, cream together the
butter and sugar with a hand mixer
until light and fluffy.

3 Beat in eggs, one at a time, mixing
well after each addition. Stir in extracts.

4 In a medium bowl, whisk together
the flour and cocoa powder and then stir

into the butter and egg mixture. Add the water and stir together until just blended.

5 Fill each liner or mold one-half to two-thirds full of batter. Bake for 12 to 15 minutes or until done.

6 Carefully remove cupcake pan from oven and place on a cooling rack for 5 minutes. Remove cupcakes from pan and place back on the rack to cool for 30 minutes before frosting and decorating.

Fresh Strawberry Cupcakes
Makes 20 to 24

1¼ cups unsalted butter, room temperature
½ cup superfine granulated sugar
6 large eggs, room temperature
2 teaspoons vanilla extract
2 teaspoons strawberry extract
½ teaspoon almond extract
3½ cups self-rising flour
½ teaspoon salt
½ cup finely chopped fresh strawberries (about 8 to 10)

1 Preheat oven to 325 degrees F. Lightly spray the inside of each cupcake liner or mold with nonstick cooking spray. Set aside.

2 In a large bowl, cream together the butter and sugar with a hand mixer until light and fluffy.

3 Beat in eggs, one at a time, mixing well after each addition. Stir in extracts.

4 In a medium bowl, whisk together the flour and salt and then stir into the butter and egg mixture. Fold in strawberries.

5 Fill each liner or mold one-half to two-thirds full of batter. Bake for 20 to 25 minutes.

6 Carefully remove cupcake pan from oven and place on a cooling rack for 5 minutes. Remove cupcakes from pan and place back on the rack to cool for 30 minutes before frosting and decorating.

Banana Cupcakes
Makes 20 to 24

1 cup unsalted butter,
   room temperature
1 cup superfine granulated sugar
4 large eggs, room temperature
2 teaspoons vanilla extract
1½ cups mashed ripe bananas
   (about 3 to 4)
2 cups self-rising flour
1 teaspoon apple pie or
   pumpkin pie spice
½ teaspoon ground cinnamon

1 Preheat oven to 350 degrees F. Lightly spray the inside of each cupcake liner or mold with nonstick cooking spray. Set aside.

2 In a large bowl, cream together the butter and sugar with a hand mixer until light and fluffy.

3 Beat in eggs, one at a time, mixing well after each addition. Stir in vanilla and bananas.

4 In a medium bowl, whisk together the flour, spice, and cinnamon and then stir into the butter and egg mixture.

5 Fill each liner or mold one-half to two-thirds full of batter. Bake for 15 to 20 minutes.

6 Carefully remove cupcake pan from oven and place on a cooling rack for 5 minutes. Remove cupcakes from pan and place back on the rack to cool for 30 minutes before frosting and decorating.

Red Velvet Cupcakes
Makes 20 to 24

1 cup canola oil
1¼ cups superfine granulated sugar
2 large eggs, room temperature
2 teaspoons vanilla extract
1 (1-ounce) bottle liquid red food dye
1¾ cups self-rising flour
¼ cup cocoa powder
¼ teaspoon salt
¾ cup buttermilk
1 teaspoon baking soda
1¼ teaspoons vinegar

1 Preheat oven to 350 degrees F. Lightly spray the inside of each cupcake liner or mold with nonstick cooking spray. Set aside.

2 In a large bowl, cream together the oil and sugar with a hand mixer until well blended.

3 Beat in eggs, one at a time, mixing well after each addition. Add vanilla and red food dye and stir to blend.

4 In a medium bowl, whisk together the flour, cocoa powder, and salt. Gradually stir the flour mixture and buttermilk into the egg mixture, first adding some flour then adding some buttermilk and repeating that pattern until both ingredients have been incorporated into the batter.

5 Mix the baking soda and vinegar in a small bowl and then stir into the batter.

6 Fill each liner or mold one-half to two-thirds full of batter. Bake for 15 to 20 minutes.

7 Carefully remove cupcake pan from oven and place on a cooling rack for 5 minutes. Remove cupcakes from pan and place back on the rack to cool for 30 minutes before frosting and decorating.

Frosting Recipes

Each frosting recipe should make enough to frost 24 cupcakes.

Buttercream Frosting

4 cups powdered sugar, or more
    if needed
Pinch of salt
¼ to ½ cup half-and-half
    or whole milk
½ cup unsalted butter,
    room temperature
1 teaspoon vanilla extract
½ teaspoon almond, coconut,
    strawberry, or raspberry
    extract (optional)
Paste food coloring (optional)

1 Place powdered sugar and salt in a large bowl and mix with a whisk to break apart any lumps.

2 Add half-and-half or milk and slowly mix with a hand mixer on low. Add butter and turn the mixer to high speed. Beat until fluffy. You may need to add a little more milk if the mixture is too thick or a little more powdered sugar if the mixture is too thin.

3 Turn hand mixer to low. Beat in vanilla and additional extracts or food coloring if using.

Chocolate Buttercream Frosting

Follow the recipe for Buttercream Frosting, but add ¼ cup cocoa powder to the dry ingredients.

Meringue Buttercream Frosting

Follow the recipe for Buttercream Frosting, but add 1 tablespoon meringue powder to the dry ingredients. If you're not going to use this frosting right away, keep it at room temperature, covered, to prevent it from developing a dry crust on top. Store any leftover frosting, covered, in the freezer for up to one month or in the refrigerator for up to one week.

Cream Cheese Frosting

1 (8-ounce) package cream
    cheese, room temperature
6 tablespoons unsalted butter,
    room temperature
3 cups powdered sugar
2 to 4 tablespoons heavy
    whipping cream
Pinch of salt
2 teaspoons vanilla extract

1 In a large bowl, combine the cream cheese and butter and beat with a hand mixer until light and fluffy.

2 Add powdered sugar and cream, beating until desired spreading consistency is reached.

3 Add salt and vanilla and beat until smooth and creamy.

Whipped Cream Frosting

1½ cups heavy whipping cream
2 teaspoons vanilla extract
2 to 4 tablespoons powdered sugar

1 Place the cream, vanilla, and powdered sugar in a large mixing bowl. Stir to combine. Cover bowl and chill both the bowl and the beaters of a hand mixer in the freezer for 10 minutes.

2 Remove bowl and beaters from freezer and beat mixture on high until stiff peaks form.

Chocolate Whipped Cream Frosting

Follow the recipe for Whipped Cream Frosting, but add 2 tablespoons cocoa powder and an additional 2 to 3 tablespoons powdered sugar.

Raspberry or Strawberry Whipped Cream Frosting

Follow the recipe for Whipped Cream Frosting, but beat cream only until soft peaks form. Then slowly add ½ cup seedless raspberry or strawberry jam while mixing. Continue beating until stiff peaks form.

Pink Princess

Favorite Vanilla
  Cupcakes (page 8)
Pink paste food coloring
Buttercream Frosting
  (page 12)
Assorted pink sprinkles
  and candies
1 pound vanilla candy
  coating or almond bark

Makes 24 cupcakes

1 Line two cookie sheets with waxed paper and spray with nonstick cooking spray. Set aside.

2 Make cupcakes according to directions, adding a small amount of pink paste food coloring to batter before baking; cool.

3 Make frosting according to directions, adding a small amount of pink paste food coloring.

4 Frost cupcakes and decorate with sprinkles and candies. Set aside until ready for wands.

5 To make wands, melt the candy coating according to package directions. Let cool 10 to 15 minutes.

6 Spoon small portions of the melted candy coating into a small ziplock bag. Seal shut and snip off one corner with kitchen scissors. Squeeze candy coating out of bag onto the prepared cookie sheets to form a wand

with a five-pointed star. Begin with the star shape first and extend the coating downward to form the wand, making each about 4 inches long. Make sure the length of the wand is fairly thick. Decorate with sprinkles. Repeat until you have made one wand for each cupcake. (You may want to make a few extra in case they break when removing them from the cookie sheet.)

7 Place cookie sheets with wands in the freezer to chill, uncovered, for 15 minutes. Remove from freezer. Carefully remove each wand from the cookie sheet and insert into the center of each decorated cupcake.

15

Tiara Princess

Choco-licious Cupcakes
   (page 8)
Buttercream Frosting
   (page 12)
Assorted sprinkles
   and candies
Toy tiaras for serving

Makes 24 cupcakes

1 Make cupcakes according to directions; cool.

2 Make frosting according to directions. Frost cupcakes and decorate with sprinkles. Serve in a toy tiara.

Lollipop

Choco-licious Cupcakes
  (page 8)
Buttercream Frosting
  (page 12)
Pink paste food coloring
Assorted candies
Whimsical lollipops

Makes 24 cupcakes

1 Make cupcakes according to directions; cool.

2 Make frosting according to directions, adding pink paste food coloring.

3 Frost cupcakes and decorate with candies. Insert lollipops into each cupcake.

17

Cotton Candy

Favorite Vanilla
  Cupcakes (page 8)
Meringue Buttercream
  Frosting (page 12)
Blue or purple paste
  food coloring
Assorted rainbow-
  colored dragées
Decorating sugars
2 bags purchased
  cotton candy

1 Make cupcakes according to directions, adding a small amount of paste food coloring to the batter.

2 Make frosting according to directions. Frost cooled cupcakes.

3 Sprinkle cupcakes with dragées and decorating sugars. Place a small amount of cotton candy in the center of each frosted and decorated cupcake.

Makes 48 mini cupcakes

Rainbow Princess

Favorite Vanilla
  Cupcakes (page 8)
Purple, blue, green,
  yellow, orange, and red
  paste food coloring
Meringue Buttercream
  Frosting (page 12)
Decorating sprinkles

Makes 24 cupcakes

1 Make cupcake batter according to directions. Divide batter into six small bowls and tint each bowl with one of the paste food colorings.

2 Place a dollop of each colored batter, in the following order, into each prepared cupcake mold or liner: purple, blue, green, yellow, orange, and red. With a wooden skewer draw a "figure 8" in the batter of each cupcake to swirl the colors. Bake and cool.

3 Make frosting according to directions. Divide frosting among six small bowls and tint each bowl with one of the paste food colorings. Cover and set aside until ready to use.

4 Place each frosting color in separate ziplock bags and seal shut. Snip one bottom corner off each bag with kitchen scissors. Frost 4 cupcakes with purple, 4 cupcakes with blue, 4 with green, and so on until you have used all six colors and all the cupcakes are frosted. Decorate with sprinkles.

Garden Princess

Fresh Strawberry
Cupcakes (page 9)
Flower-shaped
cupcake molds
Wilton precolored fondant
for flower decorations

Makes 24 cupcakes

1 Make cupcakes in flower-shaped cupcake molds according to directions; cool.

2 Make frosting according to directions. Frost cooled cupcakes.

3 Using a knife or tiny cookie cutters, cut out flower shapes and petals from fondant and assemble flowers on top of cupcakes.

Sunshine Princess

Banana Cupcakes (page 10)

Cream Cheese Frosting
   (page 13)

Pink, orange, and yellow
   paste food coloring

Yellow, red, and orange
   licorice, cut into
   3-inch pieces

Assorted colors of tube
   decorating gels

Makes 24 cupcakes

1 Make cupcakes according to directions;
   cool.

2 Make frosting according to directions.
   Divide among three bowls and tint each
with one of the paste food colorings. Frost
cooled cupcakes with the different colors of
frosting.

3 Decorate cupcakes by inserting
   8 licorice pieces into the sides of each,
going around in a circle at the upper outside
edge. This makes the rays of sunshine. Use
decorating gels to make the eyes and smiling
mouths for the sunshine faces.

Ice Cream Sundae

24 flat-bottomed ice
    cream cones
Fresh Strawberry
    Cupcakes (page 9)
1 quart vanilla ice cream
1 bottle purchased "Magic
    Shell" chocolate coating
Rainbow-colored sprinkles
1 bottle (8 ounces)
    maraschino cherries
    with stems

1. Place two muffin pans on cookie sheets. Place ice cream cones in muffin cups; set aside.

2. Make cupcake batter according to directions. Fill each prepared ice cream cone one-half to two-thirds full and then bake as directed in recipe. Cool cupcakes in pan for at least 1 hour.

3. When ready to serve, top each cupcake cone with a scoop of ice cream. Top with chocolate coating, sprinkles, and a cherry. Serve immediately.

Makes 24 cupcakes

Pink Lemonade

1 quart vanilla ice cream
2 packets presweetened
   pink lemonade mix
Pink paste food coloring
Favorite Vanilla
   Cupcakes (page 8)
   or Fresh Strawberry
   Cupcakes (page 9)
24 decorative straws,
   cut in half

Makes 48 mini cupcakes

1 Remove ice cream from freezer and allow to thaw for about 20 minutes. Scoop softened ice cream into a large bowl and stir in 1 packet of pink lemonade mix and a small amount of pink paste food coloring. Blend well and return to freezer for 2 hours or overnight.

2 Make cupcakes according to directions, adding 1 packet pink lemonade mix to batter before baking; cool.

3 To serve, place a tiny scoop of pink lemonade ice cream on top of each cupcake. Insert a cut straw into each cupcake. Serve immediately.

Pink Snowballs

Fresh Strawberry
   Cupcakes (page 9)
3 egg whites, room
   temperature
¼ teaspoon cream of tartar
4 tablespoons sugar
½ teaspoon vanilla
Pink paste food coloring
1 bottle (16 ounces)
   chocolate syrup

Makes 24 cupcakes

1 Make cupcakes according to directions; cool. Place on two cookie sheets and set aside.

2 Place egg whites in a mixing bowl and whip with a hand mixer until frothy. Add cream of tartar and beat until soft peaks form. Gradually add sugar. Add vanilla and pink paste food coloring. Continue to beat until smooth and shiny, about 2 to 3 minutes.

3 Preheat oven to 500 degrees F. Spread the meringue over the top of each cupcake on one cookie sheet. Make sure that the meringue forms a blanket over each cupcake so the cupcake top is completely covered.

4 Bake until golden brown, about 1 to 3 minutes. Watch very closely as they will brown quickly! Repeat for second pan of cupcakes. Store undecorated in the refrigerator for at least 1 hour and up to 3 hours.

5 Right before serving, drizzle each cupcake with chocolate syrup.

Frosty Ice Cream Sandwich

Choco-licious Cupcakes
  (page 8)
1 quart strawberry, vanilla,
  or mint chocolate
  chip ice cream
Assorted sprinkles

Makes 24 cupcakes

1 Line two cookie sheets with foil and spray lightly with nonstick cooking spray. Set aside.

2 Make cupcakes according to directions; cool.

3 Carefully remove cupcakes from liners or silicone molds. Place cupcakes on prepared cookie sheets. Cut each cupcake in half horizontally.

4 Cut container away from the ice cream so that you can cut ice cream into slices that are about 1 to 2 inches thick. Place a slice of ice cream on a chilled cutting board and then, using a cookie cutter, cut out a round piece about as big around as each cupcake. Place an ice cream slice on the bottom half of each cupcake and then replace the top.

5 Roll edge of ice cream in sprinkles. Cover cupcakes and place in freezer for 2 hours or overnight.

Glass Slipper

Powdered sugar for
   rolling out dough
1 roll purchased refrigerated
   sugar cookie dough
Slipper-shaped
   cookie cutter
12 craft sticks, cut in half
Red Velvet Cupcakes
   (page 10)
Meringue Buttercream
   Frosting (page 12)
Assorted colors of paste
   food coloring
Assorted sprinkles, colored
   sugars, and small colorful
   candy decorations

Makes 24 cupcakes

1 Preheat oven to 375 degrees F. Line two
cookie sheets with foil and lightly spray
with nonstick cooking spray. Set aside.

2 Lightly dust a work surface with
powdered sugar. Divide cookie dough
into thirds and roll each portion to ½ inch
thickness. Cut out with cookie cutters to make
24 cookies. Insert a craft stick into the bottom
of each cookie. Carefully place cookies about 3
inches apart on prepared cookie sheets.

3 Bake cookies for 8 to 10 minutes, or
until lightly browned. Remove from
oven to wire racks and cool for 15 minutes.
Undecorated cookies may be covered and
stored frozen for up to one month.

4 Make cupcakes according to directions;
cool. Make desired colors of frosting
for cookies and cupcakes. Frost and decorate
cookies. Generously frost cooled cupcakes.
Insert a decorated cookie into the center of
each cupcake.

Fairy-Tale Fortune

Choco-licious Cupcakes
(page 8) or Red Velvet
Cupcakes (page 10)
½ pound vanilla candy
coating or almond bark
24 purchased fortune
cookies
½ pound chocolate candy
coating or almond bark
Assorted colored sprinkles
Meringue Buttercream
Frosting (page 12)
Chocolate Buttercream
Frosting (page 12)
Pink paste food coloring

Makes 24 cupcakes

1 Line a cookie sheet with foil and lightly
coat with nonstick cooking spray.
Set aside.

2 Make cupcakes according to directions;
cool.

3 Melt vanilla candy coating according
to package directions. Remove from
heat and cool 10 minutes. Dip one-half of
12 fortune cookies into the melted candy
coating. Roll in sprinkles and place on
prepared cookie sheet. Place in freezer for
15 minutes to chill and harden. Repeat with
chocolate candy coating and remaining
fortune cookies.

4 Make frostings according to directions.
Add pink paste food coloring to the
Meringue Buttercream Frosting. Frost half the
cupcakes with chocolate frosting and half with
pink frosting. Place one decorated fortune
cookie in the center of each.

Be My Cupcake

Red Velvet Cupcakes
(page 10)
Heart-shaped silicone liners
Cream Cheese Frosting
(page 13)
Pink paste food coloring
Heart-shaped candies
and sprinkles

Makes 24 cupcakes

1 Make cupcakes in heart-shaped silicone liners according to directions; cool.

2 Make frosting according to directions. Divide between two bowls. Add pink paste food coloring to one bowl.

3 Frost cooled cupcakes. Pipe edges of pink-frosted cupcakes with white frosting and white-frosted cupcakes with pink frosting. Decorate with heart-shaped candies and sprinkles.

Cool Peppermint

Choco-licious Cupcakes
   (page 8)
Cream Cheese Frosting
   (page 13)
48 red peppermint
   candies, crushed
24 red peppermint
   candies, whole
24 Red Hots

Makes 24 cupcakes

1 Make cupcakes according to directions; cool.

2 Make frosting according to directions, but use shortening in place of butter and clear vanilla extract in place of vanilla so the frosting is snowy white if desired.

3 Frost cooled cupcakes and sprinkle with crushed peppermint candies. Top with a whole peppermint candy. Put a little frosting in center of each candy and top with a Red Hot.

39

Teacup Treats

24 ovenproof teacups
Banana Cupcakes (page 10)
Whipped Cream
   Frosting (page 13)
Fresh raspberries
Chocolate sprinkles

Makes 24 cupcakes

1 Spray the insides of ovenproof teacups with nonstick cooking spray and place on two cookie sheets.

2 Make cupcake batter. Fill prepared teacups two-thirds full and bake according to directions; cool.

3 Make frosting according to directions. Frost cooled cupcakes. Garnish with raspberries and sprinkles.

Fairy Princess Hat

1 pound vanilla candy
   coating or almond bark
24 sugar ice cream cones
Assorted sprinkles and
   small colorful candies
Tubes of decorator's frosting
   in different colors
Favorite Vanilla
   Cupcakes (page 8)
¼ cup rainbow sprinkles
Buttercream Frosting
   (page 12)
Paste food coloring in
   different colors
Fruit by the Foot

Makes 24 cupcakes

1 Line two cookie sheets with foil and lightly spray with nonstick cooking spray. Set aside.

2 Melt candy coating according to package directions. Remove from heat and cool 10 minutes. Place ice cream cones on prepared cookie sheets, open side down. Dip bottom half of each cone into candy coating and decorate using candies, sprinkles, and decorator's frosting. Put cookie sheets in freezer to chill for 15 minutes; remove.

3 Make cupcakes according to directions, folding rainbow sprinkles into the batter after it is completely mixed.

4 Make frosting according to directions. Frost cooled cupcakes and place one candy-coated ice cream cone, open side down, in the center of each cupcake.

5 Cut out strips of Fruit by the Foot to make a little pennant to add to the top of each princess hat.

Kiss Me Cupcakes

Favorite Vanilla
    Cupcakes (page 8)
Pink, green, and yellow
    paste food coloring
Buttercream Frosting
    (page 12)
1 bag (14 ounces) Wilton
    Candy Melts
Frog candy mold
Black and pink tube
    decorating gels

Makes 24 cupcakes

1 Make cupcakes according to directions, adding enough pink paste food coloring to the batter to make it bright pink.

2 Make frosting according to directions. Put one-fourth of the frosting in a separate bowl and add enough pink paste food coloring to make it bright pink. Add green and a little yellow paste food coloring to the remaining frosting.

3 Following the directions on the Candy Melts, make 24 candy frogs using the candy mold.

4 When you are ready to assemble the cupcakes, frost them green to resemble a lily pad and then set a candy frog in the center. Use black gel to make the frog's pupils and pink gel to make his mouth. Pipe bright pink frosting around the edge of the cupcake and put one star of frosting next to the frog.

45

S'mores

Choco-licious Cupcakes
(page 8)
Chocolate Buttercream
Frosting (page 12)
2 cups mini marshmallows
1 box Teddy Grahams
Small kitchen torch
(optional)

Makes 24 cupcakes

1 Make cupcakes according to directions; cool.

2 Make frosting according to directions and frost cooled cupcakes. Add a layer of mini marshmallows around the edge of each cupcake. Pipe chocolate frosting around the upper edge of the marshmallows. Insert 6 or 7 Teddy Grahams, facing outward, to make a teddy bear "crown" on top of the cupcake. Add a few more marshmallows in the center of the teddy bear crown.

3 With an adult helper, carefully toast the edges of your mini marshmallows, if desired, using a small kitchen torch. Serve immediately.

Magical Mermaid

Favorite Vanilla
   Cupcakes (page 8)
Pink paste food coloring
Buttercream Frosting
   (page 12)
Greenish-blue paste
   food coloring
24 purchased white
   chocolate seashell candies
Decorative seashell cupcake
   liners (optional)

Makes 24 cupcakes

1 Make cupcakes according to directions, adding a little pink paste food coloring to the batter.

2 Make frosting according to directions, adding a little greenish-blue paste food coloring.

3 Frost cooled cupcakes and top each with a white chocolate seashell candy. Serve in decorative liners if desired.

Bubblegum

Choco-licious Cupcakes
(page 8)
Buttercream Frosting
(page 12)
½ teaspoon bubblegum
flavoring
Candy for decorating

Makes 48 mini cupcakes

1 Make cupcakes according to directions; cool.

2 Make frosting according to directions, adding bubblegum flavoring.

3 Frost cooled cupcakes and decorate.

Enchanted Crystal Cakes

**Fresh Strawberry
   Cupcakes (page 9)**
**Meringue Buttercream
   Frosting (page 12)**
**Assorted colors of
   rock candies**
Assorted decorating sugars

Makes 24 cupcakes

1 Make cupcakes according to directions;
cool.

2 Make frosting according to directions.
Frost and decorate cooled cupcakes with
rock candies and decorating sugars.

Birthday Cupcake

Fresh Strawberry
   Cupcakes (page 9)
Chocolate Buttercream
   Frosting (page 12)
Wilton precolored fondant

Makes 6 cupcakes

1 Make mini cakes according to directions using 12 (4-inch) cake pans.

2 Make frosting according to directions. Frost 6 cakes, top side only. Place a second cake on top of each frosted cake. Frost entire layered mini cake.

3 Using one color of fondant, cut out 3 strips, about 8 inches long and 1 inch wide. Then cut out 1 strip, about 2 inches long and 1 inch wide. Using a round cookie cutter, cut out assorted colors of fondant in $1/2$- to 1-inch circles.

4 To "wrap" your birthday cupcake with a frosting bow, place 2 of the strips of fondant crossing over the top and sides of the cake. Take the third strip and fold ends up and over to form a bow.

5 Take the smaller 2-inch strip and wrap around the bow, seam side down. Place bow on the top center of the cake and secure with decorator frosting if needed. Finish decorating birthday cupcakes by placing fondant circles on the top and sides of cake.

Wild Thing

Choco-licious Cupcakes
(page 8)
1 container purchased
vanilla frosting
Black, orange, and brown
tubes of decorator's
frosting

Makes 24 cupcakes

1 Make cupcakes according to directions, using animal print cupcake liners.

2 Frost cooled cupcakes with white frosting. Use decorator's frosting to make zebra and leopard patterns on cupcakes.

Pixie Princess

Banana Cupcakes (page 10)

Cream Cheese Frosting
(page 13)

Purple paste food coloring

48 purchased candied
violets or fresh edible
flower petals

Makes 48 mini cakes

1 Make cupcakes according to directions;
cool.

2 Make frosting according to directions.
Divide between two bowls and add a
small amount of purple paste food coloring to
one to make it pale lavender.

3 Pipe frosting onto cupcakes and place
a candied violet or edible fresh flower
petal in the center of each.

Cupcake Pops

Red Velvet Cupcakes
  (page 10)
24 craft sticks or
  lollipop sticks
1 pound vanilla candy
  coating or almond bark
Assorted sprinkles
Ribbon (optional)

Makes 48 cupcake pops

1 Line two cookie sheets with foil and lightly spray with nonstick cooking spray. Set aside.

2 Make cupcakes according to directions; cool.

3 Once cupcakes are cool, remove liners and insert a craft stick into the center of each cupcake. Place on the cookie sheets, and place cookie sheets in freezer for 2 hours.

4 Melt candy coating according to package directions. Remove from heat and cool 10 to 15 minutes.

5 Remove cupcake pops from freezer and spoon candy coating over each, then decorate with sprinkles. Return to cookie sheets and chill, uncovered, in refrigerator for 1 hour before serving. Tie a ribbon to each craft stick, if desired.

Pretty Pink Shortcake

Strawberry Whipped Cream
    Frosting (page 13)
2 purchased frozen
    pound cakes
Fresh strawberries, sliced

Makes 24 cupcakes

1 Arrange 24 pink or silver cupcake liners on two cookie sheets.

2 Make frosting according to directions and keep refrigerated until ready to use.

3 Thaw pound cake and slice into pieces about ½ inch thick and then cut into squares that will fit nicely into the cupcake liners. Or cut pieces into flower shapes with a 2-inch cookie cutter.

4 In each liner, place a piece of pound cake, a dollop of frosting, and sliced strawberries. Repeat layers and serve immediately.

Crown Princess

Favorite Vanilla
   Cupcakes (page 8)
¼ cup pink sprinkles
Cream Cheese Frosting
   (page 13)
Pink paste food coloring
Dragées
Additional pink and white
   sprinkles for decorating
Decorative crown liners

Makes 24 cupcakes

1 Make cupcakes according to directions, folding ¼ cup pink sprinkles into the batter after it is completely mixed.

2 Make frosting according to directions, adding pink paste food coloring.

3 Frost cooled cupcakes and decorate. Serve in crown princess cupcake liners.

More books in the
Pink Princess series

Collect them all!